CRAFTS FOR ALL SEASONS

CREATING WITH
MOSAICS

Important Note to Children, Parents, and Teachers

Recommended for children ages 9 and up.
Some projects in this book require cutting, painting, gluing, and the use of small materials. Young children should be supervised by an adult. Due to differing conditions, individual levels of skill, and varying tools, the publisher cannot be responsible for any injuries, losses, or other damages that may result from use of the information in this book.

Published by Blackbirch Press, Inc.
260 Amity Road
Woodbridge, CT 06525

©2000 by Blackbirch Press, Inc.
First Edition

Originally published as: *Adorna con Mosaico* by Anna Freixenet.
Original Copyright: ©1995 Parramón Ediciones, S.A., World Rights, Published by Parramón Ediciones, S.A., Barcelona, Spain.

e-mail: staff@blackbirch.com
Web site: www.blackbirch.com

Printed in Spain

10 9 8 7 6 5 4 3 2 1

Library of Congress Cataloging-in-Publication Data

Freixenet, Anna.
[Adorna con mosaico. English]
Creating with paper / by Anna Freixenet.
    p.   cm. — (Crafts for all seasons)
Summary: Provides instructions for making a variety of items with mosaic decorations including treasure jewels, a button soccer ball, pencil holder, and raggedy clown.
ISBN 1-56711-440-7 (hardcover : alk. paper)
1. Mosaics—Technique—Juvenile literature. 2. House furnishings—Juvenile literature. [1. Mosaics—Technique. 2. Handicraft.]
I. Title II. Crafts for all seasons (Woodbridge, Conn.)
TT910 .F74 2000
738.5'6—dc21
00-008588
CIP
AC

Contents

| = Adult supervision strongly recommended |

CRAFTS FOR ALL SEASONS

CREATING WITH
MOSAICS

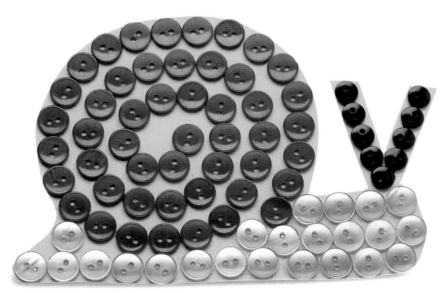

BLACKBIRCH PRESS, INC.

WOODBRIDGE, CONNECTICUT

Precious Pendants

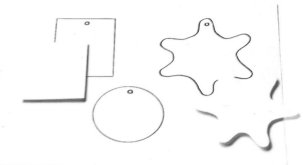

1. Draw some pendant shapes in pencil on construction paper and cut them out.

☛ *YOU'LL NEED: beads and gems, construction paper, string or yarn, a pencil, paper hole punch, glue, and scissors.*

2. Draw an arrangement of gems on each of the pendant shapes.

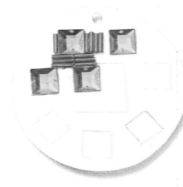

3. Use the pattern to glue the beads and gems to the construction paper pendant.

4. Punch a hole at the top of each pendant. Thread string or yarn through the hole and tie the ends in a knot. You've made your own precious treasure!

Flashy Fish

☛ **YOU'LL NEED:** *construction paper, a pencil, glue, aluminum foil, and colored tissue papers.*

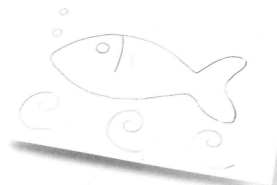

1. Draw a fish on construction paper.

2. Make tiny balls from aluminum foil and tissue paper.

3. Glue the foil balls to the inside of the fish outline, so the fish shimmers. Use black balls for the eye, gills, or mouth.

4. Fill in the background with blue balls for water and white balls for bubbles. Now you've got a bubbly fish to hang anywhere!

Panda Pal Book Covers

1. Draw the front of a panda or other animal on the front cover of a notebook.

2. On the back cover, draw the back of the panda or other animal.

3. Cut strips of colored paper.

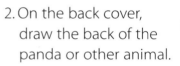

4. Cut the strips into small squares, like confetti.

6

5. Glue the confetti to form the panda and its background on both covers.

6. Fill in the front and back covers completely. It doesn't matter if the paper squares overlap.

7. When the covers are done, seal them with transparent adhesive plastic.

💡 **Use your imagination:** *You can cover all kinds of things with great square colors. How about a shoebox to hold your special treasures? Or an old oatmeal carton for a piggy bank?*

Tubby Turtle Paperweight ✂

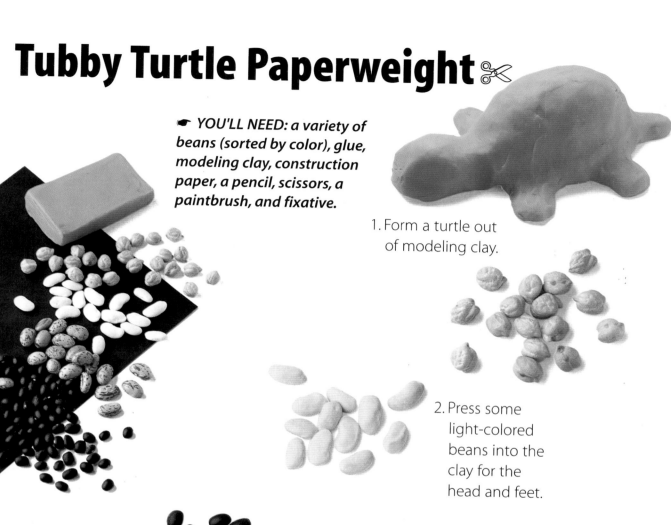

☛ YOU'LL NEED: *a variety of beans (sorted by color), glue, modeling clay, construction paper, a pencil, scissors, a paintbrush, and fixative.*

1. Form a turtle out of modeling clay.

2. Press some light-colored beans into the clay for the head and feet.

3. Press darker colors of beans into the clay for the shell.

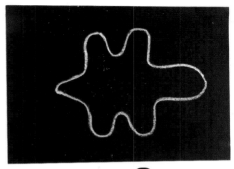

4. Place the turtle on construction paper and trace its outline.

5. Cut out the shape and glue it to the bottom of the turtle. This way the clay won't stain your papers!

6. Have an adult help you coat the turtle with a fixative to make it hard and shiny.

7. Once your turtle has dried, it is ready to hold down your important papers.

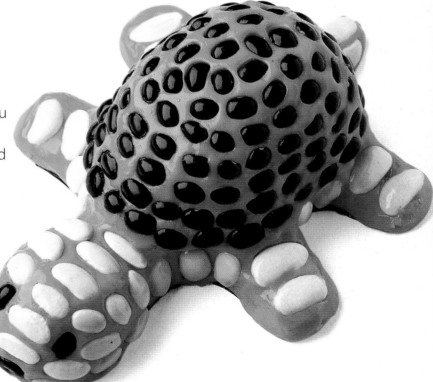

💡 **Use your imagination:** *Think up some other animals to create. Birds, butterflies, lizards, and baby seals are just a few of the many creatures you can make!*

Best Button Ornaments

☞ **YOU'LL NEED: colored construction paper, glue, a pencil, ribbon, different-colored buttons, and scissors.**

1. Draw a circle on construction paper and cut it out. Divide the circle into different sections with a pencil, as shown.

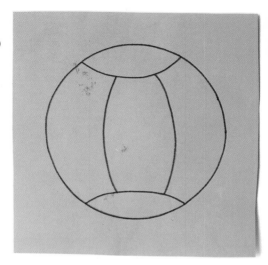

2. Glue different-colored buttons to the different sections of the circle.

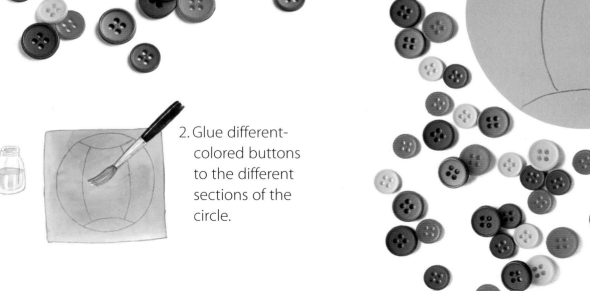

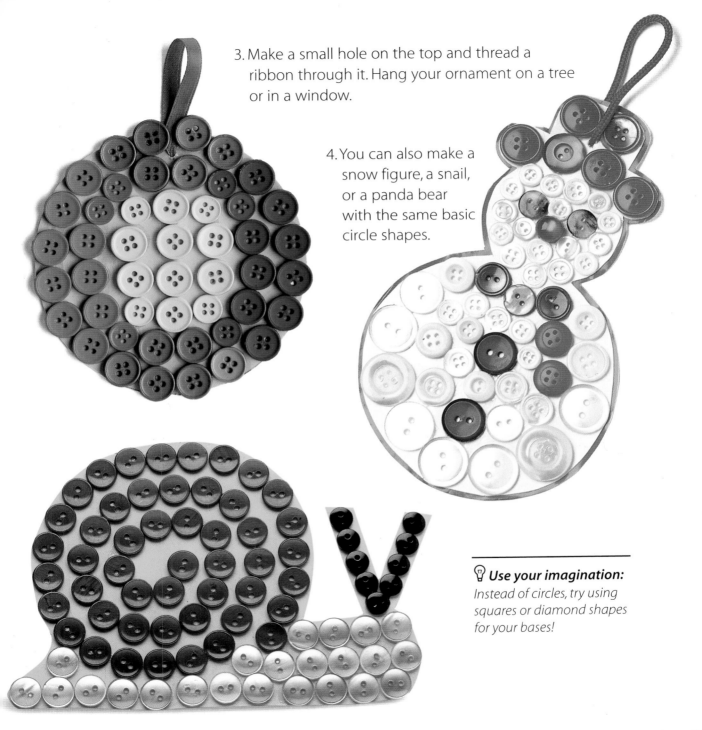

3. Make a small hole on the top and thread a ribbon through it. Hang your ornament on a tree or in a window.

4. You can also make a snow figure, a snail, or a panda bear with the same basic circle shapes.

💡 *Use your imagination:*
Instead of circles, try using squares or diamond shapes for your bases!

Funtime Flowerpot ✂

☞ YOU'LL NEED: *small stones, modeling clay, a paintbrush, and fixative.*

1. Make a ball out of modeling clay.

2. Hollow out the center to form a flower pot.

3. Smooth the sides of the pot, both on the inside and outside.

4. Lightly press small stones into the clay around the outside of the pot. You can also press shells, dried pasta, or even coins into the clay.

5. Have an adult coat the bowl with fixative.

6. Once the pot is dry, fill it with a bouquet of flowers.

💡 Use your imagination:
What other shapes would work for a pot? Try a long, thin shape or a free-form shape. Fill your container with paper clips, marbles, or loose coins.

13

Crazy Cat Mat

☛ **YOU'LL NEED: coffee beans, grains of dried corn and rice, thick construction paper or cardboard, an adhesive hanger, a pencil, glue, and scissors.**

1. Draw a cat or other animal on cardboard or thick construction paper.

💡 **Use your imagination:**
You can outline any shape or design instead. Then fill it in with different colors, shapes, and sizes!

2. Apply glue to the animal figure and fill it in with coffee beans and corn.

3. Use rice to make whiskers for the cat.

4. Apply glue to the background and cover it with grains of rice.

5. Use coffee beans to make a frame for your picture.

6. Place a hanger on the back of the picture, and it's ready for exhibition!

DuBOIS

Mystery Mask

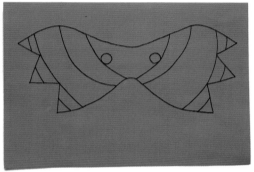

1. Draw a mask on construction paper.

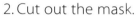

☛ **YOU'LL NEED:**
construction paper,
colored stickers, an
elastic band, a pencil,
markers, and scissors.

2. Cut out the mask.

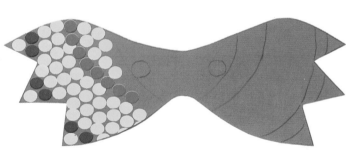

3. Form bands of colors with the stickers. Cut out two holes for the eyes.

4. Make small holes at each end and run an elastic band between them.

💡 *Use your imagination: You can also make a mask that is larger and covers your whole face. Use stickers to make the eyebrows, eyelashes, and mouth!*

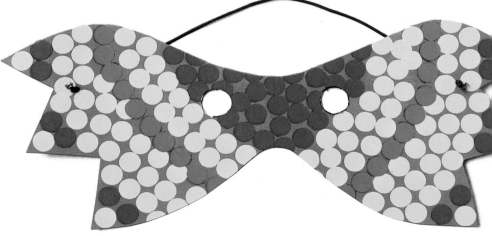

A Sneaky Snake

☞ YOU'LL NEED:
construction paper, colored stickers, a piece of ribbon, a pencil, and scissors.

1. Draw a snake on construction paper and cut it out.

2. Place stickers on the snake so that they look like scales.

3. If you like, use stickers to create a pattern on the snake's skin.

4. Glue a ribbon to the underside of the snake's mouth to make a tongue. But watch out! It might bite!

💡 *Use your imagination:* You can use cardboard and stickers to make all sorts of creatures. Try making a fish or a lizard. Use metallic stickers or small bits of foil to create shiny skin!

Super-Seedy Pencil Holder

☞ **YOU'LL NEED:**
colored construction paper, a toilet paper roll, sunflower seeds, colored markers, glue, and scissors.

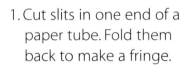

1. Cut slits in one end of a paper tube. Fold them back to make a fringe.

2. Draw a circle on construction paper that is larger than the fringed end of the tube. Then cut it out.

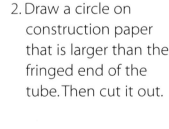

3. Glue the fringed end to the center of the construction paper circle.

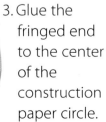

4. Color the seeds with bright markers.

5. Glue the colored seeds to the tube in rows or in a design you create.

6. Glue seeds to the base.

7. Place your favorite pencils in the holder and keep them on your desk, so they'll always be at hand.

💡 *Use your imagination:* Make several different heights of containers and glue the sides together. Fill them with dried flowers for a centerpiece, or use it as a great desk organizer!

A Cloth-Covered Clown

☞ *YOU'LL NEED:*
scraps of material, a
pencil, construction
paper, glue, string,
and scissors.

1. Draw a clown on
   construction paper.

2. Cut out small pieces of cloth.

3. Apply glue to the drawing and cover it with pieces of cloth.

4. When the glue is dry, cut out the clown.

5. Make a small hole at the top and attach string. If you like, hang your clown on the doorknob of your room!

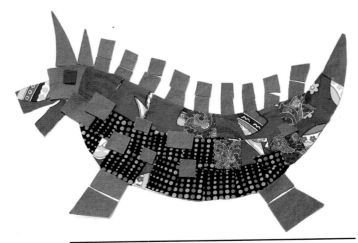

💡 *Use your imagination:* *What other things could you make from cloth? How about dinosaurs, a gingerbread figure, or your favorite stuffed animal?*

Colorful Candleholders ✂

● *YOU'LL NEED: modeling clay, a rolling pin, a blunt knife, a toothpick, two rulers, a candle, marbles, a paintbrush, and fixative.*

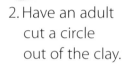

1. Flatten a piece of clay with a rolling pin. Use rulers to keep the clay an even height.

2. Have an adult cut a circle out of the clay.

3. Mark the shape of a star or another favorite shape on the circle with a toothpick.

4. Stick a candle in the center of the star to make an opening that will be the right size for the candle.

5. Have an adult help you cut out the star with a blunt knife.

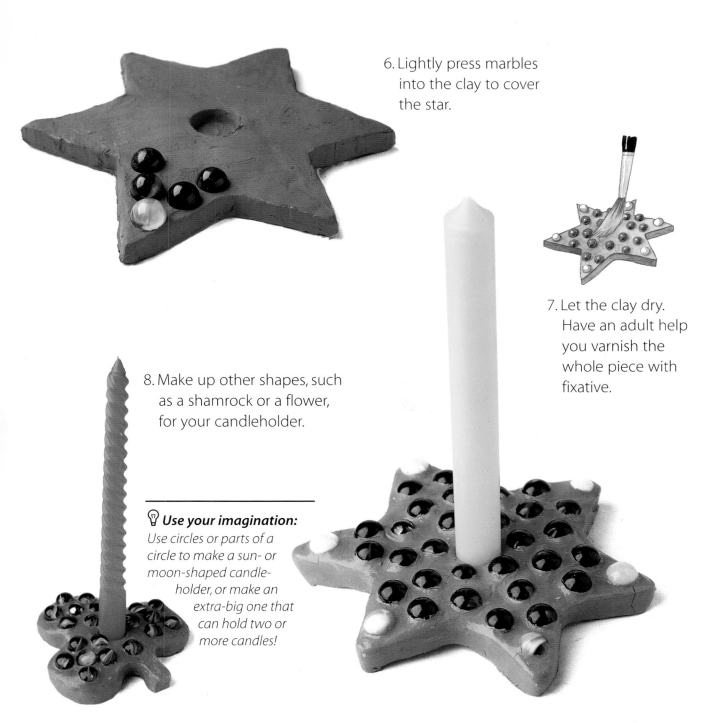

6. Lightly press marbles into the clay to cover the star.

7. Let the clay dry. Have an adult help you varnish the whole piece with fixative.

8. Make up other shapes, such as a shamrock or a flower, for your candleholder.

💡 *Use your imagination:*
Use circles or parts of a circle to make a sun- or moon-shaped candle-holder, or make an extra-big one that can hold two or more candles!

Chicken Shell-abration

☞ *YOU'LL NEED: a piece of construction paper, eggshells, a red marker, acrylic paints, a pencil, a paintbrush, and glue.*

1. Draw a hen and her chick in pencil, chalk, or crayon on construction paper.

2. Wash the eggshells inside and out and let them dry completely.

3. Break the eggshells into smaller pieces. Paint the outsides of some brown and some yellow.

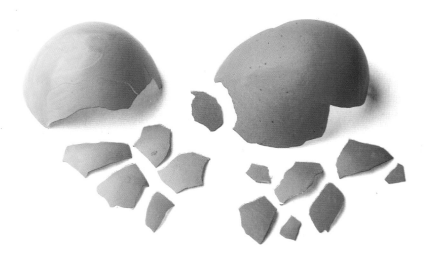

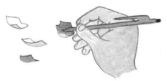

4. Use a red marker to color the inside of a few pieces of eggshell for the crest and beaks.

5. Cover the drawing with glue and stick on pieces of shell. Add black dots for eyes. And there you have it! Even the chick has broken through its shell!

💡 *Use your imagination:*
You can mix shells with beans, paper, or any other material to make a wild mix of textures and colors!

Pasta Maze Vase

☛ *YOU'LL NEED: dried pasta in different shapes and colors, a small plastic bottle, modeling clay, and a toothpick.*

1. Gather together a variety of pasta shapes.

2. Cover a small plastic bottle with modeling clay.

3. Use a toothpick to draw a design in the clay.

4. Lightly press pasta into the clay following your design.

5. Try to cover most of the clay with pasta pieces.

6. Add flowers and a little water to your wonderful pasta vase!

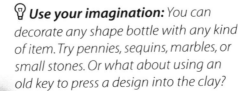

💡 **Use your imagination:** *You can decorate any shape bottle with any kind of item. Try pennies, sequins, marbles, or small stones. Or what about using an old key to press a design into the clay?*

Tack-Time Foto Frame ✄

☛ *YOU'LL NEED: two sheets of cork, thumbtacks, glue, a favorite photograph, a ruler, a pencil, an adhesive hanger, and a utility knife.*

1. Cut out two rectangles from a sheet of cork.

2. With an adult, pick out a favorite photograph and glue it to the center of one piece of cork.

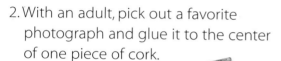

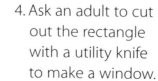

3. In the center of the other piece of cork, draw a rectangle the same size as the photo.

4. Ask an adult to cut out the rectangle with a utility knife to make a window.

5. Glue the two pieces of cork together so that the photo can be seen through the window.

6. Draw a design on the front of the frame.

7. Have an adult help you make a design using thumbtacks.

8. Place an adhesive hanger on the back of the frame. Now you've got a super photo to hang!

💡 **Use your imagination:** *Try drawing the design with glue and using colored sand or glitter. You could also glue shells, beans, or dry cereal!*

WHERE TO GET SUPPLIES

Art & Woodcrafters Supply, Inc.
www.artwoodcrafter.com
Order a catalog or browse online for many different craft supplies.

Craft Supplies
www.craftsfaironline.com/Supplies.html
This online craft store features many different sites, each featuring products
for specific hobbies.

Darice, Inc.
21160 Drake Road
Strongsville, OH 44136-6699
www.darice.com
Order a catalog or browse online for many different craft supplies.

Making Friends
www.makingfriends.com
Offers many kits and products for children's crafts.

National Artcraft
7996 Darrow Road
Twinsburg, OH 44087
www.nationalartcraft.com
This craft store features many products available through its catalog or online.

FOR MORE INFORMATION

Books

Chapman, Gillian. *Art From Fabric: With Projects Using Rags, Old Clothes, and Remnants.* New York, NY: Thomson Learning, 1995.

Chapman, Gillian. *Autumn* (Seasonal Crafts). Chatham, NJ: Raintree/Steck Vaughn, 1997.

Connor, Nikki. *Cardboard Boxes* (Creating Crafts From). Providence, RI: Copper Beech Books, 1996.

Gordon, Lynn. *52 Great Art Projects For Kids.* San Francisco, CA: Chronicle Books, 1996.

King, Penny. *Animals* (Artists' Workshop). New York, NY: Crabtree Publishing, 1996.

Newby, Nicole. *Cool Clay.* Mahwah, NJ: Troll, 1996.

Ross, Kathy. *The Best Holiday Crafts Ever.* Brookfield, CT: Millbrook Publishing, 1996.

Smith, Alistair. *Big Book of Papercraft.* Newton, MA: Educational Development Center, 1996.

Video

Blue's Clues Arts & Crafts. Nickelodeon. (1998).

Web Sites

Crafts For Kids
www.craftsforkids.miningco.com/ mbody.htm
Many different arts and crafts activities are explained in detail.

Family Crafts
www.family.go.com
Search for crafts by age group. Projects include instructions, supply list, and helpful tips.

KinderCrafts
www.EnchantedLearning.com/Crafts
Step-by-step instructions explain how to make animal, dinosaur, box, and paper crafts, plus much more.

Making Friends
www.makingfriends.com
Contains hundreds of craft ideas with detailed instructions for children ages 2 to 12, including paper dolls, summer crafts, yucky stuff, and holiday crafts.

INDEX